A Brief History of Camerto

Camerton or Camelertone as it was once k scenery, it is situated roughly 7 miles from believed to have ran along the approximate parish. Artefacts and remains of the Roman ⸺ ⸺axon period have been found in various locations during several organised excavations over the years. Roman settlements are understood to have extended to Wellow on one side and to Temple Cloud on the other. A large Saxon cemetery was revealed not far from the Fosseway; indicating a settlement probably after the Romans had left. Camerton has an ancient history of which it may be very proud.

Farming – Camerton was a farming community, many of the local farms would have been owned by the manor, the squire of the day would have leased these to local families. By law the farmers would have had to help support the up-keep of the church, by paying the rector a tythe. This was a form of tax, they would pay a percentage of their income or produce. It was good for the church but a great loss to the farmer. The tools were crude and work was hard until the early 1900s when there was a agriculture revolution. Improved horse drawn machinery, and eventually steam tractors etc; this saved hard labour and helped farming become more efficient. When the Camerton Court estate was broken up and sold, it gave local families a chance to buy their farms.

St Peter's Church – The Church is a good example of restoration and conservation, it holds much that is ancient and interesting.

St Peters Church

It is believed the monks of Glastonbury built a chantry chapel near or around the north side of St Peter's church in the late 1200s or early 1300s. A catholic priest would have sang or shouted a chantry (mass for the dead) or (obiit) latin "he has departed". Some rich landowners, guilds, societies and private donors endowed a chantry chapel with either lands, rents or assets usually left in their will. The income would have maintained the priest to carry out his chantry duties. The mass was for the founder(s) well being on earth and for their soul after their death.

Over the centuries chantries increased in wealth, King Henry VIII disapproved of the church having so much power, he ordered dissolution of the monasteries in England and Wales. In 1547 chantries were abolished and their assets were sold to people who were associated with the King.

The tower and part of the nave is believed to have been built at the end of the 15th or beginning of the 16th centuries. The church would have originally had a chancel, a nave without aisles, a western tower and a north porch.

It is not clear when St Peter's church was first built, it has evolved over a number of years with various extensions and alterations.

Reverend John Skinner

by Dave Gallop

Reverend John Skinner was one of the most renowned rectors of St Peter's church and served from 1800 to 1839. He was a learned antiquarian, an artist, poet, scholar and dutiful county priest.

Reverend John Skinner was born in 1772 into an upper class family in Bath, he was associated with the gentry of the day. He was educated at Trinity College Oxford, graduated BA in 1794 and MA in 1797 and trained to be a lawyer; had a change of heart and decided to take Holy orders and was ordained as a priest in 1799. Reverend John Skinner entered the harsh world of a Somerset coalmining village 'Camerton' in 1800. He married Anna Holmes in the summer of 1805; they had 5 children within 6 years.

Reverend John Skinner is best known for his journals, he kept a diary of everyday life in Camerton, it clearly dictates no mercy or love shown to him. He was continuously at odds with farmers and trades people; falling out over tythes due. His background was one of order and discipline; in Camerton he was faced with drunkenness, immorality and indiscipline. Tragically being left a widower with a young family to care for. He had suffered great family loss and was terribly misunderstood, smoking opium to help relieve his depression. Sadly, after 40 years of feuding with family, friends and villagers; his convictions being ridiculed and his abhorrence of the growing influence of the Methodists, he could stand it no longer. Due to total despair shot himself in nearby woods.

Unfortunately, he was an educated man, living in the wrong place at the wrong time.

The Old Manor - was given to the monks of Glastonbury as far back as King Alfred. The Abbey enjoyed the benefits derived from the manor until the reign of Henry I. Abbot Herlewin who was known for his extravagance and indiscretion, wrongfully gave the manor to Sir Richard de Cottelle; In later years the manor was given back to the Abbey by the family of de Cottelle. The manor exchanged hands to many families over the years. It has been said the old manor had nothing interesting or distinctive about it.

Camerton Court – This magnificent house was built by John Jarrett in the early 1830s, it was designed by R.S Repton who gave it the classical Greek revival style; it took nearly two years to build.

Camerton Court (south side)

Ionic colonnade that supports a balustrade parapet, there are eight columns (orders). The shape of this type of column is thought to have derived from the proportions and features of a woman.

Camerton Court was ready for John Jarrett and his wife Anna to move into; in the Autumn of 1834. The house is surrounded in breath taking scenery on the southern slopes of a landscaped vale, it extends through the Cam valley eastwards towards Bath.

John and Anna never thought they would be parents and were pleasantly surprised when Anna became pregnant with their eldest daughter Anna at the age of 41.

Anna wrote a letter to her beloved brother Wathen and his wife, informing them of her wonderful news, after 14 years of thinking she would never become a mother, Anna was pregnant.

Handwritten letter from Anna to her brother Wathen dated 18th October 1837

Extract from page 2- Would you could see my darling husband's face, and hear his joyous voice.

Extract from page 3- My dearest and kind friend Lady Elizabeth has promised to be with me, in my hour of trial.

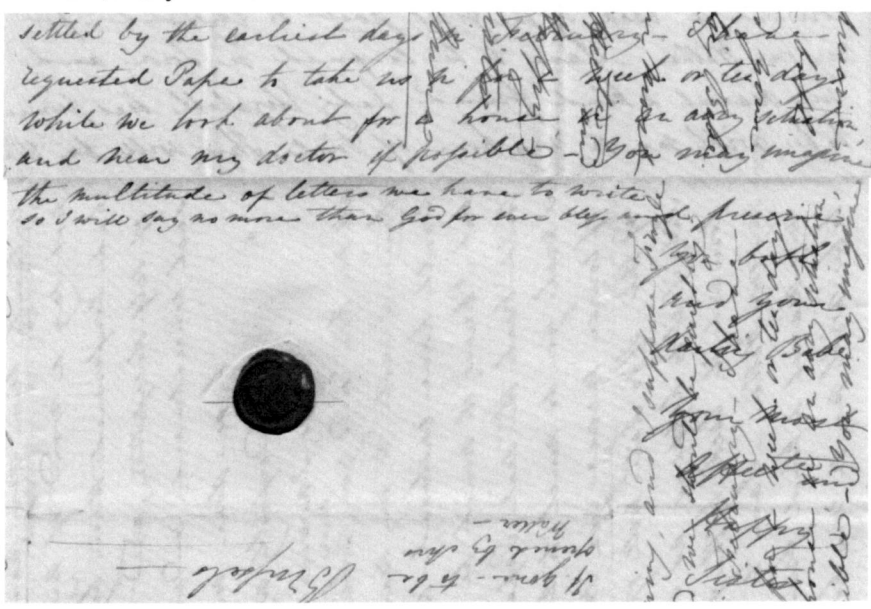

Extract from page 4- I have requested Papa to take us in for a week or ten days, for a house, in an easy situation, and near my doctor if possible. You may imagine the multitude of letters we have to write so, I will say no more than God forever bless and preserve you darling Babe.

Your most affectionate and Happy sister, Anna

Anna gave birth to their eldest daughter in 1838, after a few years she was blessed with another daughter Emily.

Portrait of Anna Jarrett   **Portrait of John Jarrett Esq**

Camerton Court (north side)

by Dave Gallop

Consists of a main block with a projecting wing on the east side. The north side has a handsome portico with a balustrade parapet on the front and two ends, supported by Tuscan columns.

The Jarrett family employed local people to work in their home and around the estate, they owned most of the land and property in Camerton as well as the mines. Camerton estate was in the hands of the Jarrett family for nearly 100 years.

There have been many owners over the years, the current owners being the Biggs family.

Local man the late Ken Biggs, purchased Camerton Court in the mid 1970s, he was a successful builder running his own company, employing hundreds of local people. His standards were high, this reflected in the work carried out. Ken, Ivy and their son Nick, worked for many years designing, creating and planting the beautiful and interesting gardens. The sketch below is just one of Camerton Court Garden's enchanting features.

Japanese Garden

by Dave Gallop

The garden derives it's beauty from mixing and blending different elements, water, rocks and natural plants with it's own beautiful surroundings. Ken's pride and joy was transforming the house from total neglect back to it's formal glory and creating the lovely gardens.

Brewery and Public Houses
The Breweries sold mainly to public houses and to private establishments. The public house sector was the back bone of the brewer's trade.

No: 2 Wick lane, Camerton

No: 2 Wick Lane - The lovely old stone cottage was the height of activity, it is believed to have been the only commercial brewery in Camerton (G.Stone & Co) it was also a local pub named 'The Rising Sun' and the village store.

Life was grim and work was hard, many used the pub as a way of release. It is hard to believe you used to be able to buy a pint and a wad of tobacco for just one penny!

A few of the old pubs that used to be in Camerton:

The Rising Sun, The Jolly Collier, Camerton Inn, Meadgate Inn and The Star Inn

The Jolly Collier

School – before Camerton C of E opened, children were taught basic education by teachers in private dwellings within the parish. For example the 'Thatched Cottage', Camerton hill was ran by the Jarrett sisters, they appointed a school mistress to teach the children to read and write; in the early 1800s (61) pupils attended. The present was founded as a parochial school (latin for parish) and later became a church of England run.

Thatched Cottage

It is believed Camerton Church School was opened in 1846 and extended in 1867. A small rural school, the building is owned by the Church of England but maintained by the County authority.

'Camerton C of E School' early 1900s

Camerton C of E School Motto is "Work hard and play hard" Class 1928

Row 4 (back row) left to right: Ernest Willcox, Henry Biggs, Lloyd Sands, Stanley Fry, Bernard Packer, not known ? and Ernest or Erick ? not known. Row 3:   ?   Millard, Olive Biggs, Dorothy Dalton, Edna Church, Eileen Church, Violet Willcox, Dorothy Leaman, Winnie Hawkins and Leslie Sperring. Row 2:   Mary Hugget, Ruby Harding, Joyce Lewis, Masey Clark, Rosie Ruddick, Eileen Sellars and Ruth Talbot. Row 1 (front row): Geoffrey Sands, ?   Willcox, Frank Atkins, Ernie Chilcot and Jack Huggett.

Mining – Camerton became a strong mining community, there were two collieries in Camerton, the first was named 'old pit' and the second 'new pit'. Old pit was also referred to as 'upper coalworks' and was sunk in the late 1780s. A better site was discovered and another pit was sunk in the early 1800s and named 'New pit'. An explosion caused by coal dust igniting, killed two men at the old pit in 1893, it was the first explosion to be ever recorded in Somerset.. Old pit closed about 1898 but remained open as an airway and escape route for new mine, also known as 'lower coalworks'. From 1888 to 1900 coal landings had doubled to over 70,000 ton per annum and receipts ranging from £17,000 to £40,000 per annum.

Camerton's Miners and Carting Boys

If you look carefully at the above photo, you will see the miner's wearing crude candles in their hats, this was the only form of light they had for working. These could be dangerous, causing explosions if they came in to contact with inflammable gases.

In the middle of the front row, a young boy is wearing a back breaking harness known as a 'Guss and Crook' tightly fitted around his waist. A (guss) was a thick rope with an iron chain and hook (crook) attached to it. The (crook) was roughly 8" long, made out of an ½" iron bar.

This picture shows an old chain and crook believed to have been used by the carting boys, currently used to tie up an old gate.

11

The chain and hook hung down the front of the waist line and would have been pushed in-between the legs, the crook would have been attached to the putt/truck. The boys would have crawled along on their hands and knees to pull the heavy putt/trucks full of coal. This method was used in Somerset until the 1930s, the main reason for this was because the seams were so narrow and no other method of hauling could be used. Boys had to haul the 5 cwt putt/truck , some times up steep inclines and at the end of their journey would have to lift the tubs using the crook on to the tracks. Until the Guss and Crook was worn in, the rope used to cut into the flesh of the young boys and burn their backs, causing terrible scars. Their 'sides' got so sore, they used to rub their own urine in, to try and harden the skin.

Accident – an extract from the 'Journal of a Somerset Rector 1803 - 1834

September 18 1805

> *A little boy of the name of Cottle, son of the schoolmistress, was killed in the coal pit by some loose ground falling upon him. He was only 8 years old and had worked a year. Surely the parents and the proprietors of the works are to blame for permitting such little boys to work, who cannot possibly take care of themselves and must be ignorant of the dangers they are exposed to' but what is not sacrificed to the shrine of covetousness ? Quid non mortalia pectora cogis. Auri sacra fames ?*

Old Pit and the Batch

1886 Map showing the 'Old Pit'

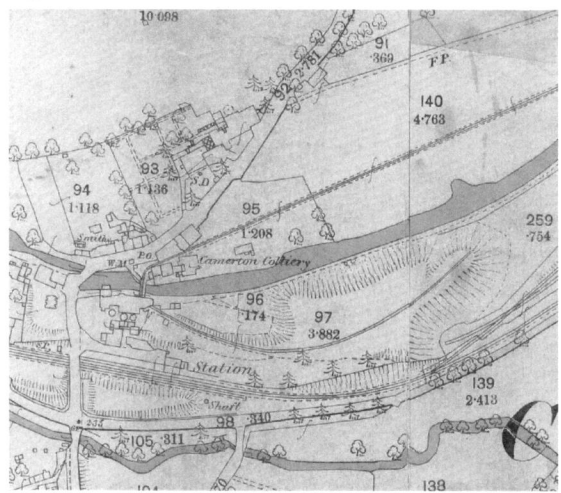

Coal and Coal dust can still be seen, in amongst the tree roots

The site of the Old Pit Head and remains of the capped Mine Shaft

The Old Batch

Above is a line of fir trees growing along the top of the old pit site and spoil or slag heap but known locally as the 'Batch'.

In 1987 local residents formed a heritage group and created the beautiful nature reserve you can see today. A wonderful haven for wildlife and a spectacular walk for all ages.

The Entrance to the Nature Reserve at the bottom of Red Hill

On the site of the old batch, over 250 steps have been built by volunteers using wooden support stakes and boards. These have been kept in good condition and made safe to use, this is thanks to local volunteers who keep the steps well maintained and occasionally have had to replace the timbers due to some being rotten and general wear and tear.

Some of the rickety steps

The colliery provided a fair wage and the coal was good quality and well sought after. Many people travelled from a far to Camerton seeking work the population increased dramatically. In 1891 it was 1,877 by 1911 it has risen to 2,386.

New Pit turned out good quality coal and produced as much as 77,000 tons of coal in a year, New pit survived to be nationalised and closed in 1950.

New Pit

The Miners Institute

The old hall was at the top of Red hill, an area known as Meadgate East, it was well supported for many years; locals can still remember dances and bands playing music there. The hall provided a wonderful venue for social events; Children's Xmas parties, the Carnival Queen and many more activities.

Xmas Party (1965)

Carnival Queen (early 1970s)

Above is Penny Fry (Carnival Queen) with her attendants, Sheridan James and Carol Pulsford .

Unfortunately the hall fell into disrepair, access was a problem so it was decided by a group of local people to construct a new building in a more suitable position. It took a huge community effort to try and get the project off the ground, a decade of fundraising.

Buy a Brick – was one of many ideas to try and raise money for the new hall

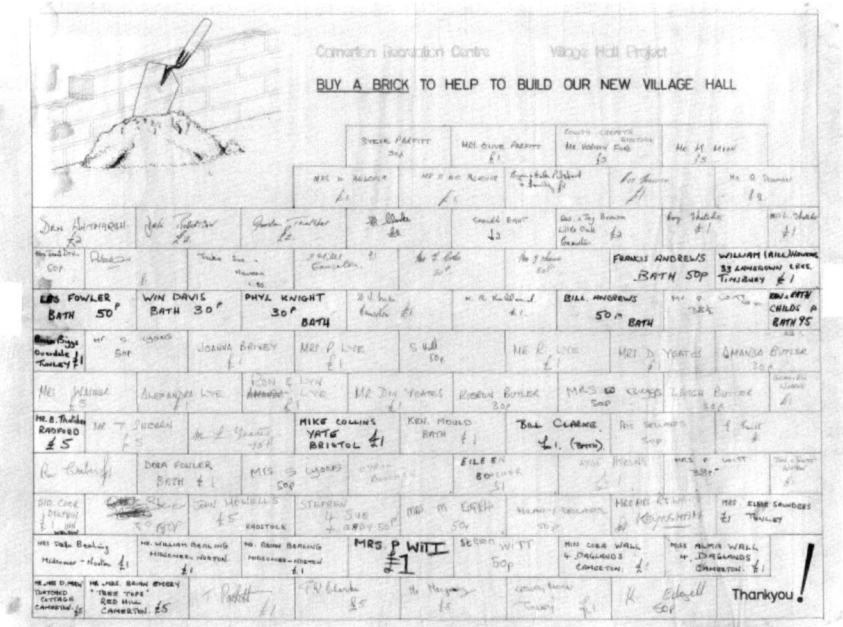

The idea of 'Buying a Brick' to raise money was Mrs Olive Parfitts, she drew up the original sheet on the back of a piece of old wall paper. Lovely lady, she couldn't get a piece of paper big enough and believed in good old fashioned improvisation. Many fundraising activities took place until eventually enough monies was raised for building work to commence. The old hall was demolished and the land was sold locally, the new purpose built 'Camerton Recreation Centre' was opened in 1980 with good access, ample car-parking space, wonderful facilities and a beautiful sports field.

Camerton Recreation Centre Aug 1980

Transportation – The local means of transportation towards the end of the 18th century would have been horse drawn carts, the roads had many steep inclines that proved difficult for horses to pull their heavy loads. The roads were poorly maintained making it an expensive form of transport.

Owners of the Somerset Mines – found it hard to compete with coal produced in the Bristol region and South Wales. Their objective was to find new markets for the Somerset coal and be able to sell their coal at a cheaper price. A few owners met up in 1792 to consider the construction of a new canal to connect their collieries to the cities of Bath and Bristol.

The Line of the Canal was determined by the famous engineer John Rennie, already working on the Kennet & Avon. In 1793 Rennie appointed Smith to take levels for the canal, two years later, Smith was appointed as surveyor to the canal.

William Smith was known as 'Strata' Smith, he made the connection between fossils and the layer of rocks they were imbedded in. It is believed that during the time he was working in the Cam valley he devised his principles on the science of Geology. He published the first Geological map of England and Wales in 1815. He was known as the 'Father of Stratigraphy' and 'Father of English Geology'.

William Smith

The Canal

In the summer of 1795 work started on the canal between Paulton Basin and Camerton. In October 1798 this section was complete and barges loaded with coal for the first time moved slowly along the canal from Camerton Coalworks to Dunkerton. In 1799 the northern branch was extended westwards from Camerton.

A Few local tragedies recorded in Journal of a Somerset rector by Howard & Peter Coombs

1803 - A stranger from Ireland, named Culling Macnab, who worked in the coal pits, much intoxicated on Saturday night was drowned by falling into the canal.

1805 – Cottle drowned himself in the canal one night after, a quarrel with his wife.

Watercolour of the Canal by Reverend John Skinner

Map showing the Canal running from Paulton Basin, through to Dundas Aqueduct

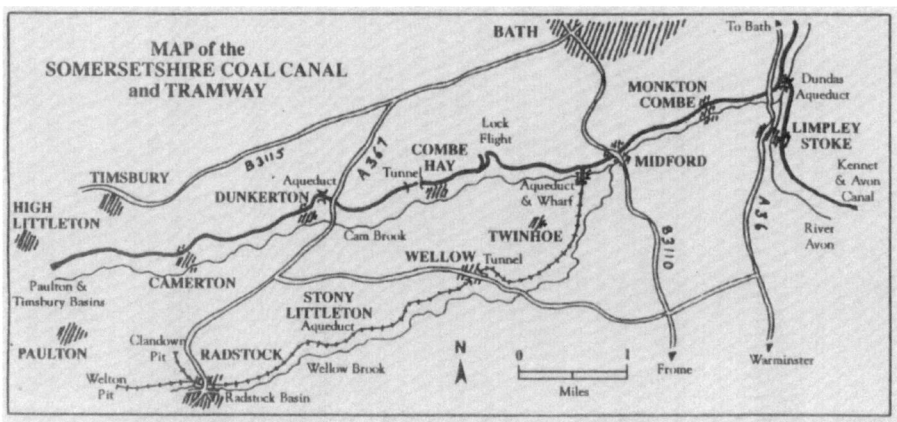

The Canal became the most successful in the country and by the 1820s it was carrying over 100,000 tons of coal per year. Unfortunately due to geological faults water loss was a major problem, from 1890 to 1893 it went into liquidation, the canal's working life ceased and was abandoned in 1898.

The Railway

In 1882 a branch line was built from Hallatrow to Camerton, in 1904 an 8 mile stretch of abandoned canal was sold to the Great Western Railway to construct the Camerton and Limpley Stoke railway.

The first section of the railway line from Camerton to Dunkerton colliery was believed to be straight forward, although it was incomplete; it opened on a temporary basis for goods traffic in April 1907. From Dunkerton the line went through the Canal tunnel at Combe Hay, it crossed the river Cam at Midford, and on through to Monkton Combe. The construction of the remaining section from Limpley stoke was a little more of a challenge and unfortunately a few accidents occurred during the time of construction; it was finally completed in 1910.

Camerton Train Station

The passenger service was withdrawn in 1914 due to the outbreak of war, however, coal trains continued to use the Camerton and Limpley Stoke railway through out the Great War; coals from the Camerton and Dunkerton colleries were of material benefit to the war effort. The passenger service was not restored until the summer of 1923, regular passenger trains ran on the branch until 1925.